because of the outpouring of love from the members at this small, Southern, African-American Baptist church.

It all began when Dr. Burnley met Sister Alice S. Crawford, who shared her love for this dying church and how it had been a part of her all her life, but she wasn't sure about the future of the church. Here, Dr. Burnley's journey to help this church in need became a vision, and immediately God's grace and mercy stepped right in!

Since that initial meeting, Sister Alice and her husband, Brother James "Butch" Crawford, have gone home to be with the Lord. However, the work of God continues on, through Dr. Burnley, driving more than 160 miles to assist this congregation. This living proof that God lives, and he lives in Dr. Burnley and the Hosannah Church family.

Through the assistance of Dr. Burnley, a new sanctuary is in its final stage of completion; a fine new pastor (Rev. Clyde Cannon) is serving as interim pastor; members are coming back to church; and God is blessing continuously. Oh, what a mighty God we serve!

— RUBY C. PRATT, church clerk, Hosannah Baptist Church

Danny Burnley has a heart for churches, especially those that are struggling. Having served as chairman of the search committee that called him to serve as our pastor, we found this out very quickly. I am looking forward to reading his book.

— WELFORD CROWE, member, West Gantt First Baptist Church

Pastors and church leaders, I want to encourage you to not give up. I have personally seen how God can take a little and do great and mighty things. Our family began visiting a small mission work in Anderson, South Carolina, in 2001. Dr. Danny Burnley had accepted the call as pastor with *only fourteen members and drove forty-eight miles one way each day. Our family joined in the summer of 2001, and in October, Danny personally led me to faith in Christ. Over the next few months, I witnessed God's blessing upon the church in many wonderful ways. God took a small group of people and made it a mighty work for God. So be encouraged, because God can do the same where you are serving today.*

— ZACH SHAW, pastor of Jones Avenue Baptist Church, Easley, S.C.

Thanks be to God for calling Danny Burnley to be pastor of Temple Baptist Church in Simpsonville, South Carolina. At the time of his calling, I served as Sunday school director. Our church was in a state of darkness, difficulty and division. Our Sunday school was disorganized, our facilities needed much renovation, our business meetings were in disorder, and we were in need of more property. What seemed to be a daunting task became a blessing for our church. God blessed the ministry of Pastor Burnley. I thank God for allowing this pastor to be a part of the legacy and history of our church. He is a great man of God and is being used of God in helping churches refocus.

— WARREN MAHAFFEY, member, Temple Baptist Church, Simpsonville, S.C.

In 1983, Union Baptist Church in Iva, South Carolina, called Danny Burnley as pastor. On the first week in May, he had scheduled a revival. As Sunday school director, I came under conviction and realized I was lost. On the night of the last service, May 8, 1983, I was saved. From Pastor Burnley's preaching and teaching the Bible and through CWT Training, Union Baptist Church grew both in spirit and in number. God has given Pastor Burnley the gift of bringing church members together and developing a vision that will challenge the church and honor God. It was truly a blessing to have him serve as our pastor.

— RHETT SIMPSON, member, Union Baptist Church, Iva, S.C.

In 1980 when I was thirteen years old, Danny Burnley came to our small church in rural Georgia. With God's guidance and Pastor Burnley's teaching and preaching the principles and instruction found in God's Word, our church began to grow both spiritually and in number. Today, our church is still a thriving church where God's love and forgiveness are found. I now serve as a deacon and Sunday school teacher of the same church. God has continued to bless our church through the hard times as well as the good times. May God bless you!

— TIM MIZE, member, Unity Baptist Church, Royston, Ga.

"Whoso findeth a wife findeth a good thing, and obtaineth favour of the Lord." (Proverbs 18:22)

I must express my love and appreciation for my wife, Laverne, who has always been by my side in ministry. As of August 9, 2015, we will have celebrated forty-six years of marriage. I thank my God for a wonderful wife and a wonderful mother to our three children.

To my children Bryan, Brooks, and Sherry:

I realize God has blessed me by having each of you to support my ministry. Sherry described our ministry best when she sat with me in a large, third-floor Sunday school classroom with only the two of us present. It was our first Sunday there. She asked, "Daddy, why do you take churches like this?" Today, we can look back and understand why. God turned that church around, and God richly blessed. Thank you, Lord Jesus, for my family!

DEDICATION

This book is dedicated to the memory of my parents, Wiley and Helen Burnley, and also in honor of my brother, James "Sonny" Burnley. Each of these suffered serious strokes in the course of their lives. Through my parents, I came to know Jesus Christ as my personal Lord and Savior. Through them I learned to love and appreciate the Church, the Body of Christ. As a result of my parents' strokes, their sufferings, their sadness and sorrows, and their continued love and commitment to Jesus Christ and His church, I learned much about spiritual strokes. Because of my love for the local church and the burden God placed upon my heart for struggling churches, I have written this book. May it be a blessing, a hope, and an encouragement to all who read it.

Helen and Wiley Burnley

FOREWORD

Having been in the ministry for fifty-three years, fifteen of which was spent traveling as a full-time evangelist, I believe I am in a position to share my observations concerning a common problem in the Southern Baptist Convention in particular and other denominations in general. The problem of which I speak is the proliferation of very weak, and sometimes dying, churches and the question of what should be done about them. The frequent answer is that these churches should simply close their doors, sell their facilities and use those funds for a new church plant. I believe in the planting of new churches. However, I do not believe that new church plants should ever be done at the expense of ending the ministries of existing churches. Additionally, it is simply a statistical fact that new church plants do not necessarily ensure that there will be a surge in new converts coming to Christ. Neither will it ensure that in a given community there will be an increase of people in that community attending church services. For example, in the Southern Baptist Convention we are seeing a boom in new church plants but a multi-year decline in church membership and baptisms.

Dr. Danny Burnley has proven by his anointed and extraordinary leadership as a pastor at churches that had at one time been identified as dying churches that these churches can once again flourish. I have been a personal witness to the effectiveness of his philosophy of ministry in turning these churches into spiritual powerhouses with dramatic increases in membership, attendance and baptisms. Most of all, these churches that once were virtually powerless with a generally pervasive mood of defeatism suddenly have burst into worship services and activities bubbling with joy and the obvious gladness of the Holy Spirit.

It is my sincere belief that this book will cause you to think with optimism about the possibilities of expanding the kingdom in a difficult church situation rather than being sucked into a gloomy concession of hopelessness. This book can be the catalyst for changing your ministry now and for the rest of your life. It is a book that has been forged in the fire of actual experiences and not by a church growth specialist who has never fought in the trenches.

Harold F. Hunter
President, Trinity College of the Bible and Theological Seminary
Newburgh, Indiana

TABLE OF CONTENTS

CHAPTER ONE
SPIRITUAL STROKES
PSALM 39:10

"Remove thy stroke away from me: I am consumed by the blow of thine hand." (Psalm 39:10)

It was around February 1965. My dad and I were sitting in our living room having a conversation about things in general. I was fifteen years old, and my dad was fifty-five years old and had been employed with the Georgia Railroad since 1943 when he was thirty-three. When he began working there, he was a fireman shoveling tons of coal on an old steam engine running from Augusta to Atlanta, Georgia, and back. At this time of our conversation, he was working as a locomotive engineer, where he had little or no exercise except when he was getting on and off the engine to have a meal.

During this particular week, my dad was not feeling well. He had taken a week of vacation thinking that he had the flu. During that week he had been to a doctor who told him that he probably had a virus. Still not feeling well, he asked my mother to call the main office of the Georgia Railroad and request another week off until he could get to feeling better. He then began to get up from where he was seated to make his way to the bedroom. As he lifted himself from the sofa, he staggered toward a close-by piano. He began moving from right to left with his hands hard-pressed against our living room wall.

I remember so clearly my mother saying to me, "Danny, your daddy has a serious problem." I agreed. My mother called my brothers, and they began making arrangements for him to see a doctor. The earliest appointment would be the next day.

After the appointment was made, my brother Tommy offered to take my dad to Washington, Georgia, some thirty miles away. After arriving, Tommy went to the passenger side of the car and opened the door. My dad's hand was frozen to the door handle. Doctors' assistants and nurses had to help my dad out of the car and into Wilkes Memorial Hospital.

That same day I was in a tenth grade typing class at Thomson High School when Tommy came to the class door and asked my teacher if he might meet with me. When I saw my brother, I knew something was terribly wrong. My brother looked at me and said, "Danny, brace yourself. I have some bad news. Daddy has had a severe stroke."

From that day until now, my life has changed dramatically. We had a Christian home. My dad was a deacon, and a Sunday school teacher, and he was so faithful to his church. Whenever he arrived home from work, his mind was always on his family, his church, and his heart was always in the Word of God. For years even until the present, I have had many questions and concerns.

Why? Why would this happen to such a man of God? Why now? All of my brothers and sisters had moved away from home. How would I handle this? Why should a mother, a stay-at-home mom, a good wife and mother to her children, and a faithful servant in the church have to experience such a terrible tragedy at this point in her life? I must admit that I was angry, confused, questioning God and having my doubts. None of this made sense!

My dad stayed in the Washington Wilkes Memorial Hospital that night. The doctors met with us and stated that they believed my dad was suffering from encephalitis, which was an inflammation of the brain caused by the bite of a mosquito. They believed that he would eventually go into a deep sleep and not wake up.

Our family decided to have him transferred to the University Hospital in Augusta, Georgia. After running many tests, doctors discovered that he had a stroke and a heart attack that was caused by a blood clot in one of his arteries. There he remained for thirty-nine days. As a fifteen-year-old being raised in a Christian home, I walked those hospital hallways questioning God and shedding many tears that no one knew about.

As a result of this stroke, he had been paralyzed from his neck down. Our pastor, Rev. Charles Lavender, called all the deacons of our church to pray for my dad. He reminded them that this man, Wiley Burnley, loved his Lord and his church. He shared with them how faithful he had been and encouraged them to fall on their knees and to lift this man of God in prayer. Each man prayed. Afterwards, when they had completed their prayers, our pastor asked them to fall on their knees again and pray with sincerity and to open up their hearts to God. This time as they prayed, tears began to fall from each of the men. They wept and agonized in prayer for my dad. This time after their prayers, my sister-in-law, Tommy's wife, knocked on the church door. When they opened the door, she shared with excitement that the doctor had called and said that Mr. Burnley had come out of much of his paralysis. This was such good news for the first time, and we now had hope of a recovery. Though much of his paralysis had been overcome, paralysis still remained on his right side.

When we brought Dad home, I helped my mother feed and clothe him, and assisted her in any way possible. He was once a strong man physically and spiritually, but now I was watching him as he had to learn to feed himself again. I watched as he so often cried like a little child. He wanted so much to walk again and to go to church again. These were the saddest days of my life.

In October of 1965, I received my driver's license. My mother was unable to drive, and due to Dad's decrease in income I had to work Monday through Friday after school at the Thomson Company that manufactured men's pants for stores throughout America. On Saturdays I worked for the A&P Grocery Store. Whenever my mom and dad had to be in Augusta, Georgia, to see their doctor, I would take them. Sometimes they would be there for hours. On several occasions my mother would come out of the doctor's office apologizing and saying how sorry she was for my having to spend my day with them. She never realized that it was such a joy to be there with them, to love them and to care for them. My heart went out to them for all they were going through.

As months passed by, my dad would ask time and time again for us to take him to church. He was almost an invalid. He would take a Ping-Pong ball in his paralyzed hand and spend hours upon hours trying to squeeze the rubber ball to help regain strength in that hand. We purchased a walker to try and help him walk again.

I shall never forget the night when there was a loud noise in our hallway. My bedroom was directly across the hallway from theirs. Whenever my mother needed me I wanted to be close. When I heard this noise, I immediately jumped out of my bed and quickly turned on my light. There in the middle of the night and in the middle of the hallway floor was my dad lying flat on his back crying like a little baby. My mother asked, "Wiley, what are you doing?" My dad answered, "I want to walk!"

After we finally helped him back into his bed and after I turned off my light and returned to my bed, I too cried. It was so difficult to see my parents going through this. Why, Lord? That was always the question.

Months passed by, until one Sunday morning as my mother and I were having breakfast together, we looked up and there in the kitchen doorway was my dad on his walker. Someway, somehow, he had dressed himself. He looked so pitiful. He had on a suit and a tie, the tie was crooked and his belt was turned. Actually, he looked half-dressed. Again, my mother asked, "Wiley, what do you think you are doing?" He answered, "I'm going to church." Slowly he made his way to the back door, trying to find a way to open it. My mother asked, "How do you think you will get there?" He replied, "I'll walk. No one will take me. I'm going to walk there!" Mother said to him, "Wiley, the doctors have told us that if you get in a crowd you may have another stroke and die." To that he answered, "That is fine. I had rather die in the house of God than any other place I know!"

That Sunday morning we helped him down our steps and into the car. When we arrived at the church, he cried. He cried entering the church. He cried as the members welcomed and hugged him. He cried when we began to sing. He cried when we prayed. He cried when the preacher preached, and he cried during the invitation. Yes, he cried — but he did not die. Yes, he cried — but the tears were tears of joy. No, he did not die. As a matter of fact, he outlived every man in his Sunday school class except one. After all he went through with his stroke and heart attack, he lived twenty-one more years and died at the age of seventy-six. He went on to be with His Lord — Our Lord and Savior Jesus Christ.

A stroke — that is what he had. The question I've always asked: Why? Why me? Why did I have to experience such sadness and heartache? Here I am today nearly forty-six years later, one out of seven children that my parents had; here I am, the least of all, preaching the Jesus Christ my parents knew so well. Why? What was God preparing me for?

Today, I submit unto you that after all these years, God has taught me much about strokes. The psalmist said that he was consumed by the stroke of God's hand. That is exactly what happens when one experiences a stroke.

You are probably asking by now, "What does this have to do with the church?" or "What does this have to do with me as a Christian?" or "Why would you want to write a book on 'spiritual strokes'?"

The answer is simple. If you were to go into the Greenville Memorial Hospital or the St. Francis Hospital here in Greenville, South Carolina, you would see signs about strokes. There are warning signs, signs with symptoms of strokes, and brochures and literature about strokes. Why? Because strokes can be prevented. Strokes are terrible experiences that affect the health, family and finances. These materials deal with physical strokes.

Today, I am a pastor. I have a pastor's heart. One day I was sitting in our living room at age fifteen and I witnessed one I loved so much who began to suffer with a stroke. Today, I pastor a church and I see those I love so dearly experience spiritual strokes. Standing before my congregation each Sunday, I watch and witness several brothers and sisters in Christ who rise from their seats and stagger, leaning on pews while making their way to their houses, unaware they are on the verge of a spiritual stroke.

Look closely at the choir, and you will see from time to time a choir member becoming a spiritual invalid. At times you will see a deacon, a teacher or other members having a spiritual stroke.

One day I received a call from Kay Jennings who was a member of our church. She shared that her husband, Gary, was having emotional problems. She went on to explain how he would continually break down and cry. Gary wanted to see me before he went to his doctor one day, and he stood near my office before he left. With tears in his eyes, he said, "Pastor, I really love you." He cried that day. As he left I thought to myself that he may have been on the verge of a stroke. He was — and he did have mini-strokes and major strokes. This was a physical stroke.

Do you remember my brother Tommy? He, too, had a stroke — but not a physical stroke. His doctor tells him that he has never seen a man in such good shape at his age. However, my brother will tell you that he has had a spiritual stroke. Remember, he was there and clearly saw my dad have a stroke. Tommy saw the symptoms and also the results of a physical stroke. At one time he had served as a deacon, but not today. Why? Because he had a spiritual stroke. There are many responsibilities within the church that he once participated in, but not now. Something in his past affected his present ministry. Somewhere as a Christian, something happened in his life and it paralyzed part of his ministry. He had suffered a partial stroke.

Standing behind my pulpit, I can point to where some believers once sat or where they once served. These persons once served faithfully, but something happened in their lives. You see, they suffered a spiritual stroke — and are no longer useful in God's kingdom work. They could continue, but they have suffered a massive stroke. There are some every Sunday that I see who are on the verge of a spiritual stroke, paralysis (partial or total) — all because of a spiritual blood clot. It is so sad. If God the Great Physician is not allowed to regain control of that life, a spiritual stroke is about to occur. If this describes you, come to God today through faith in our Lord Jesus. He can heal you of that blood clot.

CHAPTER TWO

WHAT IS A SPIRITUAL STROKE?
JOB 23:1-2

"Then Job answered and said, even today is my complaint bitter: my stroke is heavier than my groaning." (Job 23:1-2)

A wonderful door of opportunity had opened for me to preach in a week of revival services at the Keowee Baptist Church in Honea Path, South Carolina, in May 1991. We were having a blessed time, and God was moving in our midst. In the middle of that week, I received a phone call from back home telling me that my mother had been transported to the University Hospital in Augusta, Georgia. I was told that it looked very serious. Immediately I rushed to my mother's bedside. As I entered her room, family members were standing around her bed with deep concern on their faces. My mother, realizing the years we spent together caring for my dad, looked up at me with her face drawn, and with slurred speech said, "Danny, I've had a stroke just like your daddy." There we gathered around her bed, holding hands, and we prayed for our precious mother.

After sharing with my family about the revival services that were being held that week, my mother asked me to go back to

South Carolina and preach. There was no doubt in my mind as to where my parents would have me to be. Having traveled so far to be with my family and having had to leave so early, I had no time to have a meal. My sister, Marian, her husband, Gerald, and I went to Shoney's Restaurant for a meal. Gerald had never accepted Christ as his personal Lord and Savior; however, as a result of my mother's stroke and her love for her family and Lord, his heart was tender. It was there in Shoney's Restaurant where Gerald bowed his head and prayed the sinner's prayer, placing his faith in Jesus as Lord. The stroke that my mother had was heavy upon us; yet, what a joy it was to go back to that hospital and have Gerald share with her that he had just been saved! Glory to God!

As I traveled back to Honea Path that night to preach the revival service, there were so many mixed emotions. There was the spirit of joy over leading my brother-in-law to Christ. There was the spirit of sadness over my mother's stroke. Like Job, her stroke was heavier than my groaning. As I preached that night, my heart began to break and tears began to flow. It was a night I shall never forget. After the service, I received another call from home telling me that my mother had passed away. Again, I made my way back home to be with my family. Funeral arrangements were made and I was asked by my family to preach her funeral. It was an honor to be able to do so. However, my family needed to understand that I wanted to go back to Honea Path and to preach that revival; therefore, I would not be back for the receiving of friends. I returned to preach that night and the next night and then returned to my hometown to preach my mother's funeral. After her funeral service, God gave me the opportunity to preach the last night of that revival. It was a week I will never forget.

You probably understand now why God has laid it upon my heart to write a book on "spiritual strokes." God has laid so much upon my heart concerning strokes. Just as the medical doctor is concerned with people having physical strokes, so do I have a concern, as a pastor, over Christians and churches having spiritual strokes.

According to the National Stroke Association, "Blood vessels that carry blood to the brain from the heart are called arteries. The brain needs a constant supply of blood, which carries the oxygen and nutrients it needs to function. Each artery supplies blood to specific areas of the brain. A stroke occurs when one of these arteries to the brain either is blocked or bursts. As a result, part of the brain does not get the blood it needs, so it starts to die."

The human brain is divided into several areas that control movement and sensory functions, showing how the body moves and feels. When a stroke damages a certain part of the brain, that area may no longer work as well as it did before the stroke. This can cause problems with walking, speaking, seeing or feeling. An NSA illustration shows that motor and sensory functions (hand, hip, trunk, arm, fingers, face, speech, leg, head, hearing, emotions, posture, balance and coordination) can be affected by a stroke when there is a blockage or burst blood vessel. Remember that problems with walking, speaking, seeing or feeling can occur.

Now what does that have to do with spiritual strokes? Notice carefully 1 Corinthians 11:3: *"But I would have you know, that the head of every man is Christ; and the head of the woman is the man; and the head of Christ is God."*

In Ephesians 1:22-23, speaking of Christ, we read, *"And hath put all things under his feet, and gave him to be the head over all things to the church, which is his body, the fullness of him that filleth all in all."*

From Ephesians 4:15, we, the body of Christ, are told, *"But speaking the truth in love, may grow up into him in all things, which is the head, even Christ."*

Ephesians 5:23 tells us that *"Christ is the head of the church: and he is the saviour of the body."* Verse 24 follows, stating, *"The church is subject unto Christ ... ."*

Colossians 1:18 continues, *"And he is the head of the body, the church."* Colossians 2:10 follows, *"And ye are complete in him, which is the head of all principality and power,"* and 2:19 speaks of the *"Head, from which all the body by joints and bands having nourishment ministered, and knit together, increaseth with the increase of God."*

In the physical realm, there is a head. In the head, there is a brain that controls the movement and sensory functions of the body. So it is in the spiritual realm. There is the Head (Christ), where our movements and functions are controlled as His body. We have been saved by the blood of the Lord Jesus Christ. He is the Head of the Church. There is power — precious power — in the blood of the Lamb when He is in control of our body!

To have this power to speak, to hear, to move, to coordinate, to have balance, to be the healthy spiritual body that we are to be, we must understand that spiritual strokes damage our relationship to the brain (the Head of the body) and, as a result, we will no longer be able to work as well as we did before the spiritual stroke!

Remember: In the physical realm, blood vessels (arteries) carry blood to the brain (head) from the heart. Romans 10:9 is clear: *"That if thou shalt confess with thy mouth the Lord Jesus, and shalt believe in thine heart that God hath raised him from the dead, thou shalt be saved."*

The moment we put our faith in the Lord Jesus Christ, believing with our heart that Jesus Christ becomes our Head, then He has our heart! All clots are removed; the Holy Spirit has complete control. We are born again! Praise the Lord!

After our salvation, we become children of God, but impurities (spiritual blood clots) can begin to form and will lead to spiritual strokes — which result in paralysis and damage our relationship with the Head of our body. We lose our balance, our sense of direction, our ability to understand, and desire to carry out His work through our lives. My friend, that is a spiritual stroke!

What about you today? Have you allowed something to block your relationship that you once had with Christ? Are you as excited and as motivated about being a Christian and going to church as you were in the beginning? Are you as faithful in His service as you once were? Does Christ have control of your heart as He once did, or are you suffering from a spiritual stroke?

On December 20, 2010, Billy Graham was interviewed by Greta Van Susteren with Fox News. The renowned evangelist (and the most well-known evangelist in my lifetime) was ninety-two years of age. During this interview, Billy Graham shared that if he had the opportunity to live his life over again, he would do things differently. Here is the quote; "I would study more. I would pray more, travel less, take less speaking engagements. I took too many of them in too many places around the world." He said, "If I had it to do over again, I'd spend more time in meditation and prayer and just telling the Lord how much I love Him and adore Him and (am) looking forward to the time we're going to spend together for eternity."

Here was a man of God who spoke to millions over the years, and yet this great evangelist was saying, "Spend more time in study and prayer. That's the secret of successful evangelism. If you neglect that, you've neglected the very heart of God's call to you."

If Billy Graham, after all these years of successful ministry, saw this need in his life, how much more do we have this need? There is no doubt, if we would make study, prayer and spending more time with God our top priority, there would never be an experience of a spiritual stroke!

Let me encourage you to come back to the Great Physician and be healed today. Allow Him to renew your spiritual heart and health. Perhaps you are like Job with some bitter complaint and your stroke is heavier than you can bear. Then come back to Jesus and be healed.

CHAPTER THREE

WARNING SIGNS OF
A SPIRITUAL STROKE
PSALM 39:11, 13

"When thou with rebukes dost correct man for iniquity, thou makest his beauty to consume away like a moth ... . O spare me, that I may recover strength, before I go hence, and be no more." (Psalm 39:11, 13)

The psalmist, earlier in verse 10, reveals to us that he had suffered a stroke, which was actually the discipline of God in his life. In verse 11, he admits that his stroke is for his benefit in order to correct him for sin. It is the psalmist's desire to recover strength before his life is over. He realizes that the grave is not his goal, but rather a glorious anticipation awaits him. My friend, this is the proper perspective that we all should have in life. Heaven awaits us; therefore, we should desire to be clear of spiritual strokes. Just as we care for our physical health, we should be as concerned over our spiritual health.

Let us remember: Spiritual strokes will occur if we allow spiritual blood clots to develop within the body of Christ. We are His body, and He is to be the Head of our body. From this text, we see clearly that God's discipline will be sure, for He chastens His children. He loves us and empowers us when we seek to be clear of spiritual blood clots — that is, sin that so easily besets us.

In the National Stroke Association's brochure "Blood Clots and Stroke," five warning signs are listed that will prevent us from having a stroke. Let us look carefully at these from the physical standpoint and then relate them to the spiritual.

Keep in mind that a stroke occurs when a blood clot blocks an artery and keeps blood from reaching the brain. The blood clot is the result of cholesterol and other material or plaque having built up in the arteries. Also, a stroke may be the result of a blood clot traveling to your brain from your heart. Once a stroke occurs, paralysis is the result. As it is with the physical body, so it is with the spiritual body. Many Christians and churches have suffered paralysis, lack of spiritual power, confusion, disability and sadness — all because of blood clots (sin that is allowed to remain in the body). The Head is no longer in control; therefore, there develops within the body of Christ a spiritual stroke.

In order for us to prevent a spiritual stroke, let us examine closely the five warning signs of a physical stroke and see if we are not on the verge of a spiritual stroke.

The first warning sign given is sudden numbness or weakness of face, arm, or leg, especially on one side of the body. Notice that there is a numbness or weakness within the body. One of the ways you may know that you are experiencing a spiritual stroke is a realization that you have become numb or weak in the things of God. Some of you have become numb to worship. Worship is a top priority. Our Lord desires for His church to grow, for souls to be saved, for us to witness, and for us to tithe and to give our offerings. What has happened to so many in the church today? The answer is that many have grown numb to the things of God.

My oldest brother had his own construction business. He shared with me that on the morning he had his stroke, it was a beautiful day. He got out of bed, dressed for work, made it to his car. As he began to sit in the driver's seat, he realized something was wrong. There was numbness on one side. He lost control of his leg and was unable to put his key in the ignition with his right hand. By using his left hand and left foot, he was able to make it to his son's house nearby and from there he was transported to the hospital. He had a severe stroke, which began with numbness. What about you, my friend? Have you grown numb to spiritual things?

The second warning given is sudden confusion with trouble speaking or understanding. Gilbert McMullan was the deacon chairman in my church. He retired from Duke Power Company and shortly afterward he suffered a stroke that affected his speech. For a long period of time, he was unable to talk. Now some twenty years later, he is able to speak, but with difficulty doing so.

How does this relate to the spiritual body? Today, there are believers who once witnessed and testified concerning the Lord Jesus Christ. Once they had a desire to share Christ whenever and wherever possible, but today they have trouble standing in the church before family members, co-workers, and friends sharing about Christ. Why? Because of spiritual blood clots, sin has taken over their lives. Numbness over the lost and backslidden has set in. A spiritual stroke has taken, or is about to take, place. How about you, my friend? Does this describe you?

The third warning is sudden trouble seeing in one or both eyes. I have another brother nicknamed "Tootie." He is in heaven today. Before he died, there were several occasions when he informed me that he had blurred vision. Everything became milky or confusing. I am reminded of the Scripture when our Lord said, *"Lift up your eyes, and look on the fields; for they are white already to harvest" (John 4:35).* Also, our Lord said that it is not His will that any should perish but that all should come to repentance and have everlasting life. Speaking of blood clots and strokes! We know we are in trouble when we no longer have concern over lost souls. Jesus died for everyone, not just for our race or nation! However, let us listen to ourselves and look at our churches.

Years ago, a certain deacon became very negative over many things within the church. He cared so little for our children's ministry and outreach. He seemed to have had a personality change. Everyone noticed this change in his life. A few months later, it was discovered that he had a relationship with a woman outside of marriage. He then stepped down as a deacon. Over the years, this man came back to the Lord and has been restored to fellowship with this fine church. What happened to him? A spiritual blood clot was revealed. He suffered a stroke and an embarrassment before his family and church. Because of his sin (the spiritual blood clot), he could not see through his spiritual eyes.

The fourth warning is sudden trouble walking, dizziness, loss of balance or coordination. I have already shared in a previous chapter about the day my dad stood up from the sofa, grabbed the piano, leaned against the walls of our living room, and made his way slowly to his bedroom. He was dizzy, he lost his balance, and he had trouble walking. From there he had his stroke. There was a loss of balance. In the spiritual realm, we know we are having a spiritual stroke when we are out of balance. When are we in balance? It is when our priorities are in order. God is first every day of our lives. He is first when His Word is applied to our hearts as we read it daily. The Word of God and prayer are first and foremost. Our balance is in order when we love our wives as Christ loves the church and when wives love and care for their husbands. There is balance when children are brought up in the nurture and admonition of our Lord. There is balance when worship is the top priority of the family. There is balance when we care for our bodies as living sacrifices unto God by seeking to eat right and exercise. There is balance when we seek to please God in all that we do. God is in control of our finances, tithes and offerings. When anything comes before God, there is a warning. You are bound to have a spiritual stroke. Remember, Jesus said, *"My yoke is easy and my burden is light."* How is your balance today?

The fifth and last warning is a sudden severe headache with no known cause. Gary Jennings is in heaven today. He began having severe headaches, and he could not understand why. After being examined by the doctor, he discovered there were blood clots. It is amazing that there are those within the church today who look at attending church, worshipping the Lord, and singing and praising God as simply a headache — so much so that many don't want to hear the preaching of God's Word, so they stay away from God's house. Church work is a headache to many, since they are lovers of pleasure more than lovers of God. What is wrong? They are full of spiritual blood clots, and a spiritual stroke is on the way.

What is the first thing the National Stroke Association advises for us to do if we think we are on the verge of a stroke? Call 911 and get to the hospital fast! DO NOT wait for the symptoms to go away. Every minute counts.

So it is with the spiritual body! Come quickly to the Great Physician. Confess your sin to Him. Experience forgiveness and healing.

"If we confess our sins, he is faithful and just to forgive our sins, and to cleanse us from all unrighteousness." (1 John 1:9)

CHAPTER FOUR

SPIRITUAL BLOOD CLOTS
HEBREWS 12:1-6

"Let us lay aside every weight, and the sin which doth so easily beset us ... ." (Hebrews 12:1)

The writer of Hebrews tells us that there is a race before us. This is the Christian race, and we are to do whatever God has called us to do, wherever He has called us to live and move. We are challenged to run with patience and to lay aside every weight and the sin which doth so easily "beset" us.

According to the New World Dictionary, the word "beset" means "to attack from all sides; to besiege." We as Christians are attacked by the evil one constantly to hinder us and to keep us from running the race before us. He is out to kill, steal and destroy our opportunities to run this race. The word "stroke" is defined as "any attack of disease or illness, especially of apoplexy or paralysis." The "apoplexy" is a "sudden paralysis with total or partial loss of consciousness and sensation, caused by the breaking or obstruction of a blood vessel in the brain to break down, disable by a stroke."

God has saved us from sin. He has given to us His Holy

Spirit. However, in spite of everything He has provided for us, the average Christian stumbles and falls and wanders like a man who has suffered a stroke. We stumble and fall because we have been attacked by a disease called sin. A spiritual apoplexy has set in, and we experience a sudden paralysis, causing us to lose our spiritual consciousness and become disabled. When this happens, we are unable to run the race God has set before us.

The writer also tells us to *"lay aside every weight."* Weights are unnecessary in a race. A weight is a hindrance in any race. Back in the '60s there was a young man who ran in track and field. He always wanted to run barefoot. People laughed at him until they saw him winning races. He simply wanted to put aside any weight that would hinder him from winning the race.

In 1 Thessalonians 5:19, we are instructed to *"quench not the Spirit."* The word "quench" means to "extinguish, to put out, suppress or to subdue." Every believer has given his or her heart to the Lord Jesus Christ, who is the Head of the Church. Fire is one of the symbols used to depict the Holy Spirit. How do you quench a fire? You pour water on it to keep it from burning. When we quench the Spirit, we refuse to do what God wants us to do. That is, we are not listening to the Holy Spirit. We are refusing to allow the Holy Spirit to direct us. In Ephesians 4:30, the apostle Paul says, *"And grieve not the holy Spirit of God, whereby ye are sealed unto the day of redemption."* When you grieve the Holy Spirit, you grieve a person, the third part of the Trinity — the Head of the Church. When one grieves the Holy Spirit, he is allowing sin in his life, and he is stepping out of the will of God. This is a spiritual blood clot.

Remember, in the physical body, when an artery becomes blocked by plaque (the fatty substance that clogs the artery), reducing the blood flow to the brain, a stroke may occur. Paralysis follows, and the body cannot function as before. So it is with the spiritual body, the believer and the Church. When sin (the spiritual blood clot) gets between the believer's heart and the Head of the Church, the believer cannot function, nor can he run the race that God has before him.

The purpose for writing this book is to cause us to understand what is wrong with our churches. I trust that we can see why many churches have closed their doors, many are in a decline, and most are experiencing defeat and failure. What is happening? The answer is simple: Churches are having spiritual strokes.

The following is very interesting to me: transient ischemic attack (TIA). If an artery leading to the brain, or inside the brain, becomes blocked for a short period of time, the blood flow to an area of the brain slows or stops. This lack of blood (and oxygen) can cause a TIA or mini-stroke, with symptoms such as numbness, trouble speaking, and loss of balance or coordination. It is common for these symptoms to last for a very short period of time and then disappear. While TIAs cause no permanent brain damage, they are a serious warning sign of a stroke and should not be ignored. (NSA)

What is this saying? It is saying that you can know by warning signs within the body that you are about to experience a major stroke.

So it is within the spiritual body! There are symptoms that last for a short period of time — "mini-strokes." When these begin to occur, you should take action immediately by seeing your doctor (our Great Physician) and deal with this as soon as possible.

As a pastor of a church and having been in the ministry for nearly 40 years, I look out at my congregation and can see symptoms within members of our body who are on the verge of a spiritual stroke. I can see spiritual blood clots forming. The symptoms are there. When spiritual leaders within the church begin having mini-strokes, I realize that it will affect the church body. Perhaps it will be a Sunday school class, a youth department, a choir, a ministry, a deacon body, outreach, fellowship, etc. The whole body will be affected, and it is so disheartening to this pastor. In reading this book, you may realize that a spiritual mini-stroke is occurring in your life. I plead with you, return to your first love. Return to the old-fashioned altar and turn back to the One who saved you and who loves you. Please, don't experience a spiritual stroke!

My friend, you are valuable to the body of Christ:

> *"But now hath God set the members every one of them in the body, as it hath pleased him. And if they were all one member, where were the body? But now are they many members, yet but one body. And the eye cannot say unto the hand, I have no need of thee: nor again the head to the feet, I have no need of you. Nay, much more those members of the body, which*

*seem to be more feeble, are necessary: ... Now ye are
the body of Christ, and members in particular" (1
Corinthians 12:18-22, 27).*

Let me encourage every believer and every church to do as the
psalmist when he prayed, *"Search me, O God and know my heart:
try me, and know my thoughts: And see if there be any wicked way
in me, and lead me in the way everlasting" (Psalm 139:23-24).* The
psalmist wanted no spiritual blood clots to form between his heart
and his God.

What about you today? Are you concerned about sin, spiritual blood clots that are forming in your life today? Come back
to Jesus today. Do not quench the Holy Spirit. Come to the Great
Physician and experience healing and the fresh anointing of God's
Holy Spirit in your life. He is waiting, so won't you come today?

CHAPTER FIVE

CHRISTIANS WITH SPIRITUAL STROKES
ROMANS 13:14

"But put ye on the Lord Jesus Christ, and make not provision for the flesh, to fulfil the lusts thereof." (Romans 13:14)

Have you ever witnessed someone you knew and loved dearly who was vibrant, full of life and activity, vigorous, energetic, radiant, sparkling and vivacious, who suffered a stroke? If so, you would agree that this is one of the saddest experiences in life. To see someone like this become paralyzed, unable to function as they once did, and to witness their desire to have their health back is truly heart-wrenching.

To this pastor and writer, may I say that it is the same within the body of Christ. To see a pastor, deacon, staff member, Sunday school leader, teacher, singer, choir member, or any other faithful, loving, God-fearing church member suffer a spiritual stroke is just as sad.

My desire in writing this book on spiritual strokes is to help prevent a Christian or a church from having such a terrible experience. Perhaps God will use this writing to help someone who is on the verge of such a spiritual stroke to take the necessary steps to keep such an event from happening. There are some Christians already suffering from a massive spiritual stroke who need encouragement and divine restoration. My friend, God is able to do miracles in our lives. Be encouraged as you read on!

Thus far, we have learned that, as Christians, spiritual strokes damage our relationship to the brain (that is, to the Head of our body) and as a result we are no longer able to function as we did before.

Think about it: We all want our churches to grow, so we say, and we claim to have the hope that God's Holy Spirit will come down upon us in power, that souls will be saved, and that we will truly experience Him! The truth of the matter is that the Holy Spirit can leave some churches, and they will never know He departed. They will simply carry on with business as usual. If that is true, then why are we not having such experiences? The answer is spiritual strokes, which are the result of blood clots within the body of Christ.

Years ago, there was a television commercial by a fast-food restaurant where a short, elderly lady was ordering a hamburger. With her little body standing facing the cashier and with her head barely above the counter, she asked several times, "Where's the beef? Where's the beef?" This little lady had ordered a hamburger. She had the bread, lettuce, tomato, ketchup, mustard and pickle, but she had ordered a hamburger!

Today we should be asking the question within our churches,

behind our pulpits, in our deacons' meetings, in our Sunday school classes, in our worship services, at our invitations, and upon our altars: "Where's the power?" Is this not similar to the question that Elisha asked in 2 Kings 2:14 when he took the mantle of Elijah that fell from him and smote the waters and said, *"Where is the Lord God of Elijah"*? When Elisha had *"smitten the waters, they parted hither and thither, and Elisha went over."* When the sons of the prophets saw him, they said, *"The spirit of Elijah doth rest on Elisha" (2 Kings 2:15).*

So many of our churches are anemic, pale, weak, lacking vigor, ability, and are lifeless. Think about it for a moment. What is "anemia"? The dictionary defines it as a condition in which there is a reduction of the number of blood corpuscles or of the total amount of hemoglobin in the blood stream, with both resulting in such lifeless conditions!

My friend, we should heed Romans 13:11-14, where the apostle Paul admonishes the church:

> *"And that, knowing the time, that now it is time to awake out of sleep: for now is our salvation nearer than when we believed. The night is far spent, the day is at hand: let us therefore cast off the works of darkness, and let us put on the armour of light. Let us walk honestly, as in the day; not in rioting and drunkenness, not in chambering and wantonness, not in strife and envying. But put ye on the Lord Jesus*

*Christ, and make not provision for the flesh, to fulfil
the lusts thereof."*

As the church of the Lord Jesus Christ and for His sake, we
should realize that His body is full of spiritual blood clots. As a
result we have suffered spiritual strokes — paralysis, numbness,
inability to speak. We have lost our balance and coordination;
therefore, we are powerless and defeated! God wants to heal us,
restore us and empower us, so we must address our problems.
We have spiritual blood clots and spiritual strokes, so we need a
healing by the Great Physician!

If we as Christians "awake of our sleep," we will see the sad,
powerless condition in which we are existing. Simply put, we will
admit that spiritual blood clots ultimately lead to death. We must
prevent further spiritual strokes and paralysis. In our last chapter,
we began looking closely at the different types of strokes and how
the body is affected by the stroke.

First, we have examined transient ischemic attacks. As we have
discovered, these are mini-strokes resulting in numbness, loss of
balance, trouble speaking, and inability to coordinate. Remember,
these symptoms last for a very short period of time and then disappear. They are serious warning signs of a stroke and should not go
unnoticed. Now, let us look within the Church, the body of Christ.
Look carefully at a good example of those experiencing spiritual TIAs.

Consider that Sunday school leader. Do you remember
when he never missed worship services or prayer services?

Watch carefully. Do you remember when he was always present? Members of his family were key leaders and role models before others. Do you remember when he used to pray, encourage, challenge, promote, and be actively involved in so much within the church? Now you may see him occasionally in worship. Now and then he may show up for prayer service. You don't hear much from him anymore. What's happening? He is developing spiritual blood clots. He and his family have allowed the love of the world to come between his heart and the Head of the church. He no longer has time for preaching, teaching, or even reading the Word of God. He and his family are having mini-strokes. Unless he understands this and gets back to his Spiritual Doctor (the Great Physician), the warning signs are clear. He, and perhaps his family as well, are about to experience a major stroke — paralysis, the inability to function as he once did.

Second, examine the ischemic stroke. Unlike the transient ischemic attack (which lasts for a very short period of time), the ischemic stroke will cause brain cells to die. If one survives this type of stroke, he will start to have problems using certain parts of his body, or may completely lose some abilities. The ischemic stroke is the most common type of stroke, which is caused by a blood clot blocking an artery — thus cutting off the flow of oxygen-rich blood to the brain. Because blood vessels cannot deliver enough blood to the affected area, the brain cells begin to die!

According to the National Stroke Association, there are two types of ischemic strokes: embolic and thrombotic.

In an embolic stroke, a blood clot or plaque fragment forms somewhere in the body (usually the heart or in the large arteries leading to the brain), and moves through the blood stream to the brain. Once in the brain, the clot blocks a blood vessel and leads to a stroke.

In a thrombotic stroke, a blood clot that does not travel but forms inside an artery which supplies blood to the brain may interrupt the blood flow and cause a stroke.

Do you see the analogy here? If we as believers do not understand spiritual strokes and deal with spiritual blood clots, we will suffer not only from spiritual mini-strokes but instead may experience a permanent, serious paralysis. If we allow spiritual blood clots to exist, terrible consequences will follow.

Consider Willard J. (his name is not mentioned to keep from embarrassing anyone). When I served on my first nominating committee in my early twenties, I was asked to speak with Willard about a very important position within the church. He was most qualified, and he had an outstanding reputation in the church. His four children (two sets of twins) were in my Sunday school class. This brother in Christ had a beautiful wife, four precious children, a beautiful house, automobiles, property, and his family was recognized as a leading family as far as a Christian reputation was concerned.

However, when I approached him and explained why we felt he was so needed to serve in this particular position, he responded in a way I shall never forget. He said something like this: "I am going to let you younger people handle this. I've decided to take it easy this year. I'm going to sit back and take it easy."

At that time in my life I did not understand his decision, nor did I realize the symptoms of a spiritual stroke. Within the next year, he began to miss church services and was no longer active in ministry. He began missing the Word of God. It was only a matter of time when he had a relationship with another woman. He lost his wife, his children, his house, his possessions, his reputation, his witness and his influence. Here is a perfect example of a spiritual ischemic stroke. This man chose spiritual blood clots to paralyze his life and destroy the joy that he once experienced. By the end of that year, he was living out in the country in an old trailer with the other woman. Satan had sifted him *"as wheat" (Luke 22:31)*. The devil does not want you to understand spiritual blood clots. He surely does not want you to deal with them. Why? Because the blood of the Lord Jesus, the power of the Holy Spirit, will move upon us. Souls will be saved. Saints will be reconciled, the church will grow, and Christ will be glorified!

You have a decision to make. Will you be satisfied with the status quo? Will you disregard this message? Will you overlook your spiritual blood clots — or will you take action today and make your way back to our Lord Jesus, repent, and have the Great Physician heal you, empower you, and anoint you afresh?

CHAPTER SIX

SPIRITUAL BLOOD CLOTS AT EPHESUS
REVELATION 2:1-7

"Nevertheless I have somewhat against thee, because thou hast left thy first love." (Revelation 2:4)

"Come now, and let us reason together, saith the Lord: though your sins be as scarlet, they shall be as white as snow; though they be red like crimson, they shall be as wool." (Isaiah 1:18)

"Come now." God wants to bless us. The trouble we have is learning how to receive His blessings. God wants to heal our churches and to help us rebuild the walls. He even gives us the instructions as to how this can be done. In order for this to be a reality and to experience His presence and power, He wants us to respond immediately — today. When we understand that He is the Head, and we are His body, we must come to Him. Yes, we have allowed spiritual blood clots to form in our body; yet, He wants to remove them. He does not want us to suffer a spiritual stroke. My friend, we are His Church, His body, and He wants to bless us! He loved the Church and gave Himself for it.

To better understand spiritual blood clots within the Church that hinder our ministries in serving Him (the Head), let us look at a well-defined format from the book of Revelation that our Lord used in each of His letters to the seven churches.

Through the next five chapters, we will turn our attention to five of these churches that suffered from spiritual blood clots and then examine two of the churches that had no blood clots.

Notice that each of the letters is addressed to the angel of the church. The angel was the messenger whom God designated for the church. In each letter He states, *"I know thy works."* He knows if there is a spiritual blood clot and where each one is, and He lets the churches know where they are as well. Two churches — Smyrna and Philadelphia — had no spiritual blood clots. The church at Philadelphia was a very evangelistic church proclaiming God's Word; therefore, He did not see any blood clots there.

More than once in the early chapters of Revelation, as God sent His letters to the churches, He included a warning: *"He that hath an ear, let him hear what the Spirit saith."*

Since we are dealing with spiritual strokes, let us look carefully at God's Word as He points out the spiritual blood clots. We read of the church at Ephesus in Revelation 2:1-7. In verse 4 we find the blood clot: *"Nevertheless I have somewhat against thee, because thou hast left thy first love."*

Notice the blood clot. This church was once enthusiastic about Christ. The believers were once very intense and devoted to Him. Ephesus was a large city with many worldly influences drawing the

Christians away from their first love. This is exactly what happens to so many of our churches today. There are those who have allowed their home life and their church to become a burden to them. Selfish ambitions have hindered and hurt the cause of Christ, and the body has suffered. It is all because something is wrong with their relationship with Christ. Rebuilding the walls of our churches will depend upon our relationship with Christ. Any church can begin afresh through intimate fellowship with Him. Proverbs 16:7 explains it so well: *"When a man's ways please the Lord, he maketh even his enemies to be at peace with him."*

In Revelation 2:5, we are told what to do: *"Remember therefore from whence thou art fallen, and repent, and do the first works; or else I will come unto thee quickly, and will remove thy candlestick out of his place, except thou repent."* My friend, if we do not repent, we will suffer a spiritual stroke.

Notice the three "R's" in verse 5: Remember, repent, remove. The Lord tells the church first to remember. Remember when you were saved! There was joy and excitement about serving the Lord. There was a time when others followed you because they loved you and looked up to you. They did so because they witnessed your desire to please God. There was that time when you were committed, dedicated, and had so much influence. You were once recognized as an outstanding man or woman of God. Remember?

What has happened now? Why have you left your first love? Why have you become so lukewarm or cold? I encourage you, my friend, to go back to that intimate relationship with Christ.

Remember where you were in Him.

After the Lord tells the church to remember, He then instructs them to repent. To dissolve spiritual blood clots (indifference, coldness, bitterness) within the body, Christians must repent. Turn back to Him. Allow God to take away your unforgiving spirit, pride, worldly desires, attitude, and control that causes blood clots and spiritual strokes. My heart breaks over the conflicts I witnessed while I was growing up in my home church and over what I have witnessed in churches where I have been called to pastor. Through church fights, arguments, debates at business meetings and over bylaws, we have caused so many to leave our churches. We visit, call, advertise and try to be evangelistic, but when these blood clots are present, we need to stop, turn, repent and turn to Him!

The third "R" stands for remove. If we do not remember and repent, God says that He will remove our candlestick out of His place. In other words, He will remove our light. This is what has happened in the majority of our churches. The doors to many of our churches are closed. The crowds are no longer there. Blood clots have formed. Lights have gone out. Churches have lost their reputations. Our young adults have left the churches, and others have followed. The church is suffering from a major stroke.

Today, our Lord sees our situation and our condition. He knows our lights are burning so low. If we allow spiritual blood clots to continue to exist, He will turn off the light.

What about you, my friend? Are you allowing a blood clot to form near your heart? Will you allow a spiritual stroke to occur in your life that will hurt Christ's body and injure those who look up to you?

Revelation 2:7 states, *"He that hath an ear let him hear."*

Isaiah 1:18 says, *"Come now, and let us reason together, saith the Lord."* Allow the Great Physician to restore your joy. Don't allow the devil to ruin your reputation for Christ and use your spiritual blood clot to cause paralysis within the body. God loves you, and He loves His body — the Church.

Allow God to have full access to your mind and heart. Surrender to His will and to His transforming power. Return to His precious Word, for His glory.

CHAPTER SEVEN

SPIRITUAL BLOOD CLOTS AT PERGAMUM

REVELATION 2:12-17

"But I have a few things against thee ... ." (Revelation 2:14)

Religion! The city where this church was located was saturated with religion. It was filled with false teachings and different beliefs. The Lord knew exactly where this church was located, and He also knew the need for the city. Through His messenger, the angel of the church, He states, *"These things saith he which hath the sharp sword with two edges" (Revelation 2:12)*. What is He speaking of here? He is speaking of the Word of God.

God knew this was a religious but wicked city. He knew the situation that existed. In verse 13, He speaks of the believers: *"I know thy works, and where thou dwellest, even where Satan's seat is."* When I think of Greenville, South Carolina, where I have served for years, it is a very religious city. Bible schools are everywhere. False prophets and false teachings also surround us. The saddest thing to me, however, is that so many of our churches and schools have suffered spiritual strokes. The Christian influence has dwindled to an all-time low. Satan's presence is powerful here. I pray

God will heal our churches from spiritual strokes and clear the spiritual blood clots.

I thank my God for the believers in Greenville as they, like the believers in Pergamum, are faithful in their defense of the deity of Christ. To the believers in Pergamum, the Lord says, *"Thou holdest fast my name and hast not denied my faith."* He goes on to speak of Antipas as his *"faithful martyr."* Thank God for the remnant of His people who are ready to serve, and even die for, Him.

Beginning in verses 14 and 15, our Lord begins to reveal the formation of spiritual blood clots. Read carefully:

> *"But I have a few things against thee, because thou hast there them that hold the doctrine of Balaam, who taught Balac to cast a stumbling block before the children of Israel, to eat things sacrificed unto idols, and to commit fornication. So hast thou also them that hold the doctrine of the Nicolaitanes, which thing I hate."*

What was happening here? Where is the spiritual blood clot? The blood clot was in the false teaching. Because of false teaching, idolatry, fornication and other sins of the world infiltrated the church. Because there were those in Pergamum who held to the doctrine, a large spiritual blood clot had formed, and God said He hates it!

Now you may be asking, what does this have to do with us?

In order for us as the body of Christ to experience the power and presence of God, we must understand the power of the pure and precious Word of God. We cannot put too much emphasis on God's Word!

In my first church that I pastored back in the early 1980s, there were many cults in our area pushing their teachings — Sun Myung Moon, Jim Jones, the Mormons, Jehovah's Witnesses, and others. As a young preacher just entering the ministry, I thought it would be good to teach a series of classes on "cults." As I began making preparations, ordering materials and studying, an elderly pastor — Rev. Dallas Suttles, my mentor — was visiting with me, and I shared my plans concerning the class on cults. In his wisdom, he shared very gently that I should not be wasting my time studying and teaching about cults. He said to me, "Danny, teach them the Word of God. Spend your time in the Word. If you will teach your people the Word of God, they will know if it is a cult or some false teaching. Stay in the Word. Teach the Word."

My thoughts go back to a young adult Sunday school class that I taught back in the 1970s before entering full-time Christian service as a pastor. We had thirty-three faithful young adults who loved the Word of God. I remember the joy and fellowship in our Sunday school class. We simply could not get enough of the Word of God. We loved preaching, worship, and all of our services. We would even meet at homes after evening services for food, fellowship, and to study more of the Word.

It was during this time of my life that I realized a love, desire and hunger for God's Word, and a heart of joy to share God's Word and to reach others for Christ. As a young deacon chairman and as a Sunday school teacher, I left home, entered Bible college, and began preparing for ministry.

There was a young man who later became the teacher of that class. He began to move away from Sunday school literature, as he claimed to want to teach straight from the Bible. This would have been fine, but no one knew much about the young man. Eventually, class members began calling me about his teachings. These young adults realized that his teachings were those of the Jehovah's Witnesses, as he taught there was no hell and other false teachings of this cult. My advice was simply for them to share their concern with their pastor and deacon chairman. It was soon solved, and the class went forward. They knew the truth because they knew the Word. A spiritual blood clot was removed.

In 1988, a search committee approached me about becoming their pastor. This was a divided search committee and a divided church. They had been without a pastor for more than two years. The only thing they could agree on was the fact that they all wanted me to come and be their pastor. I knew they were desperate!

In this particular church, the former pastor had been accused of having committed adultery with a staff member. Families began to choose sides. The deacon body was divided. There were two churches in one as a result. They had two different types of literature. There were two different checking accounts. I could go on explaining a church full of spiritual blood clots, mini-strokes, and even paralysis. It was not my desire to get into such a disaster area.

One day I came across a very old book written many years ago by an old, experienced pastor. He shared a personal experience in his life that I shall never forget, and this has helped me in the most trying experiences of my life and ministry.

This old pastor told of the time when he grew up on a farm. His father had a chore for him to do every night before he would go to bed. It was his responsibility to go out to the old barn and check on a cow in one of the stalls. Before going out into the barn, he would always light his kerosene lantern. When he entered the barn with his light, he noticed two things would always happen: The birds that were inside the barn would start singing, and the rats would run for cover. Years later, after becoming a pastor, he noticed two things always happened when he began to preach the Word: The Christians would begin to sing, and the rats would still run for cover! Amen!

Well, I accepted the call to become the pastor of that divided church. Some members told me that they would give me six months. By God's grace, I served as their pastor for some thirteen years.

At the first deacons' meeting, a very strong resentment was present. The deacons expressed several accusations and charges concerning proposed changes that were going to be made under my pastorate. To that, I responded that no changes would be made for the first year. The deacons were asked to share with everyone they knew to bring their Bibles to every worship service, since it was my desire to simply preach the Word of God and to bring honor and glory to the name above every name — the name of Jesus Christ, the Son of God and King of Kings.

I had realized that the old preacher's book concerning the light was for this church. During that first year and following, I have sought to simply preach God's Word and to leave the results to him. The preacher was right: Christians did begin to sing, and rats ran for cover. The Holy Spirit works through the preaching of the Word of God. It is by the foolishness of preaching the Word that men are saved, and so it is with the dissolving of spiritual blood clots. Our focus must be the Word!

In another church that I once pastored, the members of the search committee informed me of their concern that the doors of the church building would soon be closed. By God's grace, He allowed me to pastor this church for eight and a half years. During those years of ministry, I noticed a common denominator describing all churches that are not growing and are in decline. It is a fact that the Word of God does not have top priority within the Church. Oh yes, they believe on the Lord Jesus Christ as Savior, and they believe the Bible to be the Word of God. However, the spiritual blood clot here is clear: The Word of God is not of utmost importance.

I remember when I first became the pastor. On Sunday mornings as I looked out the windows of my pastor's study while church members were arriving for Sunday school, there would be only about five men who would actually bring their Bibles to church.

When I asked for those in our worship service to hold up their Bibles as we prepared to read from God's Word, only a few men had a Bible. There is the spiritual blood clot. No wonder the church was in decline. Imagine trying to travel hundreds of miles to a certain destination without a road map. It would be impossible. So it is with the church. Imagine deacons, yokefellows, laborers within the church, committee personnel and others who hold prominent positions in the church, but never take their Bible to church, or a Sunday school class, or a worship service. Imagine that these are the ones chosen to be the spiritual leaders within the church. My friend, a church cannot grow with spiritual blood clots.

It is amazing to me how difficult it has been to have some members live under the Word of God. Even some worship services have been changed time and again to accommodate the carnal Christian who would rather be on some committee than to be present worshipping our Lord and feeding on the Word of God. If we will be as anxious about reading and hearing the Word of God as we are about serving on some committee or about holding some key position in the church, God will dissolve all spiritual blood clots!

If we are serious about rebuilding the walls of our churches, about souls being saved, and about church growth, then we must heed what Christ tells the church to do in verse 16: *"Repent; or else I will come unto thee quickly, and will fight against them with the sword of my mouth."* In other words, either we deal with the blood clot, or we will suffer a spiritual stroke.

The only cure for spiritual blood clots is to "repent." There must be "a change of mind." God's Word says, *"If we confess our sins, he is faithful and just to forgive us our sins, and to cleanse us from all unrighteousness" (1 John 1:9).* If the church will not repent, the Lord said He would fight against them with the sword of His mouth, which is the Word of God. As believers in Jesus Christ, we are the church, and we form what the Bible calls the body of Christ. We are to be lights in the world. If we are going to identify with the Person of Jesus Christ, then we must recognize the Word of God as our top priority and authority.

"He that hath an ear, let him hear what the Spirit saith unto the churches." (Revelation 2:17)

CHAPTER EIGHT

SPIRITUAL BLOOD CLOTS
AT THYATIRA
REVELATION 2:18-29

"These things saith the Son of God, who hath his eyes like unto a flame of fire, and his feet are like fine brass ... ." (Revelation 2:18)

Of all the seven churches in Revelation, this church, in my opinion, describes many within our Southern Baptist Convention. The reason I point this out is because of what we have witnessed over the years when we have had our battle over the Bible.

This letter to the church at Thyatira was a letter of wrath due to a terrible blood clot within the heart of the church. God's eyes penetrated this body of believers. His judgment was about to fall upon them. A spiritual stroke was about to occur. Why? Because of Jezebel, who portrayed herself as a spokesperson of God. She claimed to be a prophetess of the Lord, but instead she denied the Word of God.

Notice the blood clot that was about to produce a spiritual stroke: *"Thou sufferest that woman Jezebel, which calleth herself a prophetess, to teach and to seduce my servants"* (v. 20).

Does this not sound like our denomination, when our Bible

colleges and seminaries allowed teachers to teach, mock and belittle the Word of God? I have heard of pastors who shared that they had teachers in seminary who would actually stand on the Bible in front of a class and tell the students to forget what they had been taught about the Book, and then they would teach their false doctrines. Liberalism was a major blood clot because of false teachings. We allowed modern-day Jezebels to teach in our schools and preach in our churches. Just as the church at Thyatira was commended for her works, love, faith, service and patience, so has it been for our churches and denomination. Yes, to be a Baptist, we have to be healthy in order to attend all the meetings and activities that have so little to do with teaching the Word of God and the winning of lost souls. We are so busy, we have allowed spiritual blood clots to fill our churches. We could cut out many of our meetings and accomplish more for the glory of God. False teachings, denying the Word of God, and mingling this with what we call worship produce spiritual blood clots.

Galatians 5:9 tells us, *"A little leaven leaveneth the whole lump."* This church suffered a spiritual stroke, and so did our denomination. The teaching from this woman Jezebel is described as "the depths of Satan." Brethren, to be clear of spiritual blood clots, we should be involved in classes where Jesus is taught to be the only way to God. We should seek to feed on and grow by the Word of God and to encourage our people to be faithful in worship on the Lord's Day.

God will one day deal with this false doctrine and false

teaching. Verses 22 and 23 tell us that God *"will cast her into a bed, and them that commit adultery with her into great tribulation ... and I will kill her children with death."* This spiritual blood clot, if it continues without true repentance, will cause God's judgment to fall. It will not result in a spiritual stroke but in an eternal death.

I love to read verses 26 and 28. Here, God promises His power to grow His church, to reach the lost, to do His will if only we repent of our sins and allow Him to dissolve all spiritual blood clots.

I am so thankful that the Southern Baptist Convention has repented and has dealt with the Jezebels within our colleges and seminaries. It has been a blessing to see the numbers of students who are now in our schools, feeding on the Word of God. No, we are not perfect yet, nor will we be perfect until Jesus returns. I am thankful to be a Southern Baptist because we turned back to the Word of God!

"He that hath an ear, let him hear what the Spirit saith unto the churches." (Revelation 2:29)

CHAPTER NINE

SPIRITUAL BLOOD CLOTS AT SARDIS

REVELATION 3:1-6

"I know thy works, that thou hast a name that thou livest, and art dead." (Revelation 3:1)

The fourth church of the seven churches to receive a letter from Christ Himself is the church at Sardis. Twice in verse 1 we find the word "seven": *"These things saith he that hath the seven Spirits of God, and the seven stars."* This divine number expresses fullness and completeness. It is Christ's desire to direct His church. He is the One to be in control. Because of the presence and power of the Holy Spirit, believers can experience His power and know His perfect will as we submit to His Holy Word.

We can be assured that spiritual blood clots and spiritual strokes will definitely result when Christ is not in control. When He is no longer the Head and Lord over the Church, a spiritual stroke will surely occur.

The church at Sardis was no doubt made up of people who were willing to work and who were very organized. We know this because our Lord tells them, *"I know thy works."* He goes on to tell them, *"Thou hast a name that thou livest."* Could this not be said of a number of churches in our present day? From the outward appearance, the church looked alive and well. Many of the members of such a church look well by the clothes they wear and by their cars parked in the church parking lot. This reminds me of a church I had the opportunity to serve and to help rebuild the spiritual wall. Many people from the area would say to me, after they understood that I was the pastor, "Oh, you pastor that large church on the corner." My response was, "The building is large, but that is not the church." From the outside of the facilities, one would think that this church was a large and thriving church. The truth is, however, it only had twenty-eight people in Sunday school at the beginning of my pastorate and some thirty to forty in worship attendance.

Though this church had a reputation of being alive, the fact was that this church was as dead as last year's Christmas turkey. The Lord said, *"Thou hast a name that thou livest, and art dead."* If the Lord says the church is dead, that settles it. The members of the church probably did not think so. They were active, they were busy, they went through their religious ceremonies — but the church, according to God's Word, was dead!

We can only wonder how many churches gather on Sunday mornings and Wednesday nights that have a form of godliness but deny the power thereof. We must admit that many churchgoers do not care about Bible study. Attending church is no more than a ritual or a ceremony. Here is a church with a major blood clot. They had a name that they were living, but in reality they were dead! The spiritual blood clot had caused a spiritual stroke; therefore, the church died.

When I read from Isaiah 29:13 where God said, *"This people draw near me with their mouth, and with their lips do honour me, but have removed their heart far from me,"* it concerns me how we can be involved in religious activity and be dead! Think of the spiritual blood clots within the Church that produce spiritual strokes and even death. Consider the hypocrites in Matthew 6 who gave their offerings *"that they may have glory of men"* and even prayed *"that they may be seen of men."* There were those who would disguise their faces so that they might appear to be fasting. Why would they do such things? The answer is found in Matthew 23:5: *"But all their works they do for to be seen of men."* Where are the spiritual blood clots within the church that cause spiritual strokes and cause the church to die? They are located in the hypocrites who put on a front to appear religious.

As believers, we should understand that God is not impressed over the fact that we are a deacon, director or leader in the church, nor for our outward appearances. God fully understands who we are, why we are doing what we do, or what kind of front we may put on. He knows all about us.

You may be in such a church, asking, what can we do in our situation? Our Lord gives the answer in verse 2 when He says, *"Be watchful, and strengthen the things which remain."* To me, I see a glimmer of hope here for such a church. Our Lord goes on to instruct us in verse 3: *"Remember therefore how thou hast received and heard, and hold fast, and repent.*" What are we to hold on to? The one thing we are to hold on to is the precious Word of God.

After having been around the church now for nearly sixty-six years and having pastored churches that needed revitalization, I have learned the importance of simply preaching God's Word.

As soon as I become a pastor of such a church (or any church), the first thing I seek to do is to stress the importance of the Bible. Everyone is challenged to bring Bibles and to study these Bibles. When God's people set as their goal to put study first and foremost, the church can turn around. After preaching the Bible Sunday after Sunday during the first year as a pastor, you can tell who loves God's Word and His ways. It will be very clear.

One of the most encouraging verses concerning the church at Sardis is verse 4. Notice carefully as you read this verse: "Thou hast a few names even in Sardis which have not defiled their garments; and they shall walk with me in white: for they are worthy." Back in the 1960s, there was a song that contained the lyrics, "It only takes a spark to get a fire going and once it has begun you can wind up in its glowing. That's how it is with God's love, once you've experienced it. You spread His love to wings above, you want to pass it on!"

Over the years I have discovered that God always has that little remnant who love the Word of God and believe His Word. They are hungry to hear and heed His Word. These are the true believers within the church who have no desire to fulfill the lust of the flesh, but rather they are ready to do His will. As it was in the church at Sardis, so it is in most churches: There will be a few who make up the remnant.

Years ago early in my ministry, Dr. Harold Hunter was in revival with me. It seemed to me at that time there were some members within my church who couldn't care less about church growth. Dr. Hunter gave me some very practical and sound advice. He said, "Danny, move with the movers!" I realized then — and even more so now — that there are those who want to worship in spirit and in truth. There are those who want souls to be saved and to glorify God. They want the church to grow and to go forward. So let us encourage one another. Let us not grow weary in well doing. May God find us faithful, and let us move with the movers.

Verse 5 tells us, "He that overcometh, the same shall be clothed in white raiment; and I will not blot out his name out of the book of life, but I will confess his name before my Father, and before his angels."

God promises us that we can be overcomers. How is this possible? It is by the blood of Christ. The Great Physician can remove any and all spiritual blood clots if we will simply follow our Savior and Lord Jesus Christ.

"He that hath an ear, let him hear what the Spirit saith unto the churches." (Revelation 3:6)

CHAPTER TEN
SPIRITUAL BLOOD CLOTS AT LAODICEA
REVELATION 3:14-22

"And knowest not that thou art wretched, and miserable, and poor, and blind, and naked." (Revelation 3:17)

One of my elderly deacons shared with me back during the 1980s his opinion concerning the church today. He said something like this: "Pastor, one of the greatest problems with the church in our day is prosperity." My friend, he was right.

I have observed young couples starting out in love and humility, desiring so much to put God first in their marriage. However, over time they purchase a new car and later another new car. They purchase a house, furniture, clothes and other items on credit. They climb up what our society calls "the ladder of success," and they are able to take more vacations, with their houses becoming only a place to change clothes. The cares of the world overtake their cares for the Word of God, worship and commitment to the Lord Jesus Christ and His Church. As time passes on, the material things, the love of pleasure and a selfish attitude become the norm — and eventually the family self-destructs. Fleshly desires and the cares of the world become the head, not our Lord Jesus Christ.

So it was with the church at Laodicea. When you consider the location of this church, the spiritual blood clot and the cause of the blood clot can be clearly seen. Laodicea was a place of wealth, prosperity, industry and commerce. The marketplaces were everywhere, and prosperity filled the air. Laodicea was much like many of today's prosperous cities, where most anything that was needed was there.

The church at Laodicea appeared to be in need of nothing as well. This church from the numbers standpoint — and even from the world's view of a church — appeared to be lacking in nothing. This church looked successful perhaps because of their beautiful facilities, attendance, excellent musicians, singers, programs and activities.

Looking at this church through the eyes of our Lord in Scripture, we will find a number of blood clots. Like a young couple starting out with a wonderful marriage, so it can be with the church. Over a period of time, prosperity and possessions never fully satisfy. It is so sad to me when I see a Christian lose his or her excitement in serving our Lord. My heart breaks when a faithful Christian turns from his faithfulness and commitment to the church. Spiritual blood clots are formed when there are those who lose interest in the things of God. They hurt themselves by their testimony and witness. The church is hurt and hindered. Those who claim to be Christians and followers of our Lord Jesus Christ have become lukewarm. They have lost their fire, their enthusiasm, and their zeal. It reminds me of the church member who loved to sit by the fire. This poem was shared with a church I pastored. Evangelist Aubert Rose was leading us in a Sunday school growth revival, and it describes why many churches are in a decline or dying:

> *He wasn't much for stirrin' about,*
> *It wasn't his desire.*
> *It mattered not what others did,*
> *He kept sittin' by the fire.*
> *Same old story, day by day,*
> *He never seemed to tire.*
> *While others worked to build the church,*
> *He kept sittin' by the fire.*
> *At last he died, as all must do,*
> *Some say he went up higher.*
> *But if he's still doin' what he used to do,*
> *He's still sittin' by the fire!*

The Lord Jesus made it clear: "I know thy works." We know the Laodicean believers were involved and active. They were going through the motions that appeared "churchy." Like so many of our churches today, these believers became lukewarm — no expectation, no spiritual goals, no excitement, no enthusiasm.

Do you remember the time when you were thirsty for a glass of cold water? You turned on the faucet and out came warm water.

You would remember how sickening it was. Our Lord said that this church was neither cold nor hot. The church was so sickening to Him that He would spew them out of his mouth. A lukewarm church is filled with spiritual blood clots.

The church at Laodicea thought well of themselves, for they were full of worldly wealth. Like many churches today, their concentration was on their buildings and budgets. Since they had great facilities, huge budgets and large attendance, everything seemed so successful. The Lord Jesus calls them "wretched" and "miserable." There was no desire for the Word of God, no love for Jesus Christ, no ambition to witness to lost sinners. Their material wealth had blinded their eyes. They said of themselves, "We are rich, increased with goods, and have need of nothing." The Lord said of them, "You are poor, blind, and naked."

My friend, many churches are so much like the Laodicean church. We talk a good spiritual talk, but we are failing miserably in witnessing about God's salvation and grace. It is amazing how churches start out so well, until they become covered up with material blessings and soon lose their love for God's Word and that of reaching souls. One of the very first signs of a spiritual blood clot is when outreach and winning lost souls are put on the back burner. In our day, soul winning has become second fiddle to buildings, budgets and bylaws. Very little do we hear of churches evangelizing anymore. It is more about "me, my and mine."

The good news in the middle of the message is formed in verse 18: "I counsel thee to buy of me gold tried in the fire, that thou mayest be rich; and white raiment, that thou mayest be clothed, and that the shame of thy nakedness do not appear; and anoint thine eyes with eyesalve, that thou mayest see."

Praise God, here we find a glimmer of hope. God loves this church, and He is having compassion on them. Our Great Physician pleads with them, "Anoint thine eyes with eyesalve, that thou mayest see"!

Back when I was a teenager, Charles Lavender was my pastor. I remember so vividly how he would pray, "Lord, anoint our eyes with your eyesalve that we may see and unplug our ears that we may hear." Spiritual blood clots can create spiritual blindness. God has plenty of eyesalve for us. Keep in mind, He wants to heal our church, but we must allow Him to take control, to be the Head, and to anoint us with the Holy Spirit. He can, and He will!

Read carefully what He says to this church in verse 19 as He offers His remedy for the spiritual blood clots: "As many as I love, I rebuke and chasten: be zealous therefore, and repent."

Whatever happened to the word "repent" in our churches? God is giving us counsel here. As a church, we must repent. We must be willing to die to ourselves and let Christ reign. A senior pastor in our area has as his motto, "Get on, get off, get over, or get run over." Our Lord is saying that He will not put up with luke-warmness. If we do not get hot and be on fire for Him, He will spew us out!

Again, notice how our Lord is reaching out to this church in love. He is offering a beginning revitalization plan if someone in the church will just take heed:

> *"Behold, I stand at the door, and knock: if any man hear my voice, and open the door, I will come in to him, and will sup with him, and he with me."* *(Revelation 3:20)*

To the reader today, I plead with you to understand that you may be the spark that can cause the spiritual fire to burn again in your church. God promises to have fellowship with you as a result of feeding on His Word and knowing Him personally as your Lord and Savior.

The hope I have in regard to revitalizing any church is to study each of these churches. To each church the Lord reveals the spiritual blood clots, and He also offers a plan of action as the Great Physician. Our Lord wants you to hear His Word, and by His Holy Spirit make His Word real to you. Please, hear His voice, open up your heart's door and allow Him to remove all spiritual blood clots by His power. He will if you open your heart's door to allow Him in.

"He that hath an ear, let him hear what the Spirit saith unto the churches." *(Revelation 3:22)*

CHAPTER ELEVEN

SPIRITUAL BLOOD CLOTS AT CORINTH
1 CORINTHIANS 3:1

"And I, brethren, could not speak unto you as unto spiritual, but as unto carnal, even as unto babes in Christ." (1 Corinthians 3:1)

In order for us as believers, individually and collectively, to be a healthy body and to experience God's working power through us, we must keep spiritual blood clots from forming within our body (the Church) that will hinder our relationship with the Head (Jesus Christ). Remember, He is the Head of the Church, and we are His body. He controls the movement and functions of the body.

We have already examined five churches in Revelation that suffered spiritual blood clots and spiritual strokes. Before we begin examining the last two churches in Revelation, which had no spiritual blood clots, let us look carefully at the church in Corinth. It was filled with problems that hindered Paul and the church as well.

In Paul's letter to the church at Corinth, he is writing in response to the household of Chloe and to the report of strife in the church. After a delegation of three men were sent from the church with a letter seeking Paul's wisdom concerning questions the church had, he writes this letter known as 1 Corinthians, and later he writes another letter known as 2 Corinthians. In this first letter, he systematically addresses issues (we can call them blood clots). What are the issues? They are divisions in the church, immorality, lawsuits, those opposing Paul's apostleship, meat being offered to idols, marriage, divorce, and the Lord's Supper. These problems — or spiritual blood clots — must be addressed and dealt with, or a spiritual stroke will occur.

Paul immediately addresses these issues through his teaching on spiritual gifts (chapter 12), Christian love (chapter 13), the resurrection (chapter 15), and he also shares words of discipline to the congregation while proclaiming the Gospel. By studying 1 Corinthians, we can learn so much in revitalizing a church. This church was filled with spiritual blood clots. Pay careful attention to how Paul addresses these problems and emphasizes the answer to these difficulties. He lets the church know that it is the power of God in the preaching of Jesus Christ and proclaiming of the Gospel where we find wisdom. As believers in the church receive God's Word and as they understand the spiritual gifts for each believer, the body is built up in love.

Consider this particular church for a few moments. Corinth had become a commercial and economic center located on the Mediterranean Sea. It was a wealthy cosmopolitan center with several hundred thousand people. This had become a wicked city made up of Greeks, Jews, sailors, merchants and people from all over the world. It was full of sin and sinful influence from so many.

Religion was on every corner. Temples built for false gods were everywhere. There were priestesses who were prostitutes; therefore, sex religion had its influence. Morally unrestrained people covered the city. There was no limit to sin.

It was here in this city where Paul had previously preached the Gospel and established this church while he was there on his second missionary journey. It was not long after Paul departed when severe evils, factions and divisions began to threaten the stability and existence of the church. Does this not sound like churches of our day? Most of our churches are in decline, discouraged, divided, depressed, and feeling defeated.

The apostle Paul knew the answer to these spiritual blood clots. It is found in chapter 2:2: *"For I determined not to know any thing among you, save Jesus Christ, and him crucified."* As was the church at Corinth, many today have lost sight of the main objective. They have lost their true vision by moving away from the person of Jesus Christ. Many churches have lost sight of the lordship of Jesus Christ. Our churches are starving for the Word of God. A major problem (a spiritual blood clot) that has caused such a decline and spiritual strokes is found in chapter 3:1: *"And I, brethren, could not speak unto you as unto spiritual, but as unto carnal, even as unto babes in Christ."* The reason then and now for having many hindrances within the church is because so many believers were, and are, baby Christians. The purpose for Paul's writing was to give counsel and to correct errors that had developed in the church.

Ron Davis served as our director of missions for the Greenville

Baptist Association for some seventeen years. Our association is made up of 115 churches. He once told the pastors, that if God does not show up in some thirty to forty of our churches, they will close within five to ten years.

I know he was correct; however, I also believe God can, and will, show up if only a remnant will get right with God. If only we would humble ourselves, realize that God is ready to help, guide and direct us, He will show up! Many leaders do not want to admit it, but Christ is not in control of our churches when bylaws, budgets and buildings are our major concern. The carnality of our churches have produced spiritual blood clots and spiritual strokes. Much of our labor in the church has so little to do with true worship, growing the church, reaching the lost, and opening our doors to new ministries. There is little or no desire on the part of our carnal church members to *"go out into the highways and hedges, and compel them to come in, that my house may be filled" (Luke 14:23).* Why is this? It is because we have so many baby Christians. Just observe most of our meetings that we attend. There is constant dealing and discussion over carnal things rather than ministries and spiritual things. When was the last time your committee came together for earnest prayer, building up worship services, speaking about lost souls, and winning others to Christ? Look around at many of the churches in decline, and you will see very few men with a Bible. They may have bylaws and budget sheets with their magnifying glasses looking over these, but where is the Word of God?

In chapter 1:2, when the apostle Paul addressed the believers "at Corinth," he reminded them that they were "sanctified" — that is, set apart and "in Christ Jesus." He wanted them to know they were set apart to glorify Christ, and he called them "saints" because their faith was in the Lord Jesus Christ.

He continues in chapter 3:1-3 telling them that he could not speak to them *"as unto spiritual but as unto carnal, even as unto babes in Christ."* In verse 2, he informs them, *"I have fed you with milk, and not with meat: for hitherto ye were not able to bear it, neither yet now are ye able."* He gives the reason why in verse 3: *"For ye are yet carnal: for whereas there is among you envying, and strife, and divisions, are ye not carnal, and walk as men?"*

Does this not sound like so many of our churches? Do we not understand why we have so many churches in decline and needing revitalization? Paul gives the remedy for change, but as we look at this word "carnal," let us consider the characteristics of a baby and see what a baby Christian is.

First, we know that a baby cries a lot. My friend, you can spot a baby Christian when you begin implementing a ministry to reach more souls. It is amazing to see crybabies who will hinder outreach and growth. Very few are involved in this ministry. If some cannot have all the attention, no one else will.

Second, a baby wants his own way. He says, this is my church and I want things to remain as they are. It is mine and you can't have it.

Third, a baby is selfish. He does not want to share what is his. I could write another book on being selfish. Over the years, I have witnessed members asking visitors to move from where they are sitting because, according to the church member, "You are sitting in my seat"!

Fourth, a baby plays while others work. The baby makes a lot of noise but is never involved in work. Consider the church. Where are the saints when it comes to outreach? Where are the saints when it comes to discipleship and Bible fellowship? A baby is inclined to play while others work.

Fifth, a baby cannot reproduce. Why? Because the child has not physically matured. What is the fruit of the apple tree? Apples! What should be the fruit of a Christian? More Christians!

Sixth, a baby wastes food. Now here we can find a spiritual blood clot in the church. Put a plate before a little child and in no time he will spill the food all over the floor, have it in his hair, and all over his hands and face. This describes so many Christians. Where is our spiritual food? It is in the Word of God. Take time for a self-examination and see how much food you waste. How much of the Word of God have you taken in last week? Food is prepared for you and is available each Lord's Day. Sunday school teachers and preachers are prepared to feed you spiritually, but are you interested in the Word? Many are out playing while others are working. Many do not want to come to the table, but instead waste their food. Why? Because they are carnal! This is the major problem within our churches. No wonder our churches are in a mess and in a decline. Jesus Christ, who is the Word, is not our major focus. His crucifixion is only a brief memory when we see a cross on the wall.

Lost souls are unimportant; the study of the Word of God is unimportant; church growth is unimportant; ministry is unimportant; faithfulness, worship and spiritual maturity are unimportant.

Then what is the answer to all of the spiritual blood clots that are forming? *"As newborn babes, desire the sincere milk of the word, that ye may grow thereby: ... if so be ye have tasted that the Lord is gracious" (1 Peter 2:2, 3)*. If any church is to grow numerically, it must first grow spiritually. To grow spiritually, to dissolve spiritual blood clots, and to be healed of spiritual strokes, the Word of God must have top priority. Jesus Christ asked Peter three times, "Lovest thou Me?" Peter responded, "Lord, you know I love you." Jesus then said, "Feed my sheep." If a church will simply return to her first love, God will change things. He will change things in your life and your church. If you truly love the Lord Jesus as you say you do, you will love His Word. Jesus Christ is the Word. To love Christ is to love His Word.

The apostle Paul knew the answer to all the spiritual blood clots at Corinth. That is why he said to the church, *"For I determined not to know any thing among you, save Jesus Christ, and him crucified" (1 Corinthians 2:2)*.

CHAPTER TWELVE

CHURCHES WITHOUT SPIRITUAL BLOOD CLOTS: SMYRNA
REVELATION 2:8-11

"I know thy works, and tribulation, and poverty, (but thou art rich) ... ." (Revelation 2:9)

Up until this point, we have examined the five churches in Revelation, in addition to the church at Corinth. These churches all suffered from spiritual blood clots and spiritual strokes. Let us now turn our attention to the churches that had no spiritual blood clots. Have you noticed thus far that where the cities were located there was prosperity and ungodliness? Most people were interested in material wealth. As we examine the church at Smyrna, we discover terrible suffering and persecution they faced from the Jews.

Our Lord knew all about their sufferings and hardships. He says to the church, *"I know thy works, and tribulation, and poverty, (but thou art rich) ... ."* Stop for a moment and consider what our Lord is saying. Compare His words to our thinking. Many times we see huge, beautiful buildings, stained glass windows, and large congregations full of wealth and popularity. We say to ourselves, "This church is rich!"

I heard a pastor of a Georgia town's First Baptist Church talking about what happens at his church from time to time. He spoke of a family (representative of many today) that united with his church the previous Sunday. The man of the house was a businessman who had recently moved his family to the town. The family came in for the worship service and united with the church their first Sunday. According to the pastor, the family knew nothing about the church, their doctrine, their ministries nor the pastor. You see, the man was a businessman who united with a church without time for prayer or any other considerations. Yes, this was a fine pastor and a wonderful church. The pastor was simply sharing with his listeners that so many are looking for a church that would promote their business and bring recognition to them.

Is it not interesting that no other church that we examined thus far was told, *"Thou art rich"*? Like the church at Laodicea, many churches think they are rich. They say, as did the Laodicean church, *"I am rich, and increased with goods and have need of nothing" (Revelation 3:17)*. We look at our facilities, our wealth and even our numbers, and do not realize that we are full of spiritual blood clots and are *"wretched, and miserable, and poor, and blind, and naked" (v. 17)*. This is what the Lord said of the church at Laodicea. A church may be rich in the eyes of the world but not in regard to spiritual possessions.

As I look back over the years of my ministry, I have been blessed and fortunate to have several wealthy men within the church. In one pastorate as I was questioned by the search committee, there was one very wealthy man who asked me about my family, doctrine, plans, etc. I wondered if he would be a problem in my ministry. After serving as pastor of that particular church, I can say that there has never been a more encouraging, dedicated man than that dear brother in Christ. He never tried to control me, hinder me, nor criticize me. He was truly a man of God. I know of some pastors who have had a self-centered rich man to be a spiritual blood clot in the church and who make the pastor miserable. The Bible never says that money is the root of all evil, but rather it is the love of money that becomes the spiritual blood clot.

Since our Lord found no spiritual blood clots within the church of Smyrna, let us look carefully at this church and see why our Lord declared, *"Thou art rich."*

First, consider what our Lord says in Revelation 2:9: *"I know thy works, and tribulation, and poverty, (but thou art rich) and I know the blasphemy of them which say they are Jews, and are not, but are the synagogue of Satan."* Satan and his cronies spoke evil against the church and tried to hinder and destroy the church's reputation. The Lord said to them, *"Thou shalt suffer."* He knew what they were going through in slander, persecution and poverty. He knew they would be tried and tested. Some would be placed in prison, and some would die as martyrs. Let us not forget that He also said of them, *"Thou art rich."*

As I think about the number of churches in our denomination, my heart goes out to pastors and churches who are struggling and need revitalization. Yet, by studying the church at Smyrna, I realize

God is working in and through all of us. As we look at so many churches that appear to be "prosperous" and "successful," and then look at others that appear to be failures, we can only wonder how God sees them.

I have worked with churches and pastors who seem to have lost their dream, their vision. It has been the most wonderful joy to help some of these refocus, face their challenges and have a new hope in Christ.

The Master promised those at Smyrna to *"be faithful unto death, and I will give [them] a crown of life" (v. 10)*. Our Lord Jesus knows what we are all going through, and He cares for us. It was Jesus who was rich and who became poor that those of us who are poor may become rich.

If your church is discouraged, depressed, defeated, and has lost hope, then be encouraged by studying this church. Don't quit. Do not give up. Christ understands.

When I surrendered my life to full-time Christian service, my pastor shared some very good advice about being a pastor. He told me to be careful not to have ulcers. He informed me that there would be times when members would tell of other churches and what great things they have accomplished. I would hear about how many people were attending another church in town, or about how many were baptized in a certain church, and about the great building being built. He then said, be careful because Satan will whisper in your ear and tell you that you are a failure, and that you are not doing anything. Satan will have you so discouraged and worried, and ulcers will be the result.

Before you and your congregation decide to "throw in the towel," remember what God has done for you in the past. Deal with your present spiritual blood clots. Pray to God and wait upon Him to guide you and give you a fresh vision.

One of my most wonderful experiences in the church was when I served as a deacon in my twenties. We probably averaged around 140 in Sunday school in a small town in Georgia. We did not argue over the style of music, nor did we grow spiritually cross-eyed trying to please every person who came to town. We simply loved God and His church. We prayed together, cared for one another, sought to reach lost souls, and we simply enjoyed church!

Stop right where you are! Enjoy life. Enjoy your church. Let God have His will and way in your church. Major on the majors and not on the minors. Carry out the Great Commission. Look toward heaven. Be like Saul and just cry out, *"Lord, what wilt thou have me do?"* Your church may be a rich church and not know it. The one thing we do know about each of these churches is that God loved them and, in spite of all the spiritual blood clots, He was ready to bless them if only they would allow Him to be Lord!

CHAPTER THIRTEEN

CHURCHES WITHOUT SPIRITUAL BLOOD CLOTS: PHILADELPHIA
REVELATION 3:8-13

"I know thy works: behold, I have set before thee an open door ... ."
(Revelation 3:8)

How refreshing it is to examine the church at Philadelphia. If you want your church to become stirred again and to become excited about future goals and possibilities, then I suggest you seek to be identified with this church.

Look carefully at verse 8! Our Master says He has *"set before thee an open door."* Here is a church that has wonderful opportunities before them. So it is with any church, if we will allow God to be the Head of the church. We do not find one word of condemnation directed toward this church. Our Lord finds no spiritual blood clots. He tells them they have "little strength." Does this describe your church? Your church may be small in number and have little finances. Notice that this church, which has little strength, has God's promise that He has set before them an open door!

After pastoring Temple Baptist Church in Simpsonville, South Carolina, for nearly thirteen years, I was led to accept a call to a new mission church in Anderson, South Carolina, some forty-eight miles away. On the first Sunday with them, there were only fourteen people present for Sunday school, in addition to my wife, daughter and myself. Having accepted this call, I told my wife that this would probably end my ministry involvement with the South Carolina Baptist Convention. God, by His grace, had already opened the doors for me to serve as registration secretary, second vice president, nominating committee chairman, and other positions throughout our convention. Think about this for a moment. Here I am at this small mission work in the back of a shopping center. Who would expect me to serve anywhere at this time?

When we arrived at the next South Carolina Baptist Convention meeting in November, Dr. Jerry White stood before the convention and nominated me to serve as first vice president. Who would have ever imagined this could happen? How did this happen? God did this! He opened this door.

Consider this also: Some eleven years later, I was asked to come and help Laurel Baptist Church in Greenville, South Carolina. This church was six months away from closing its doors and selling the property to a business next door. There were only twenty-eight to thirty members attending Sunday school and only thirty to thirty-five members attending worship. The total weekly offerings were around $1,100 per week, with total missions giving for the year around $1,800. Is there anyone reading this who wants to have a pity party? Well, read on! How can a pastor make a living, provide insurance and have a church pay its overhead and repair a building that needed heat pumps, painting, roof repairs, remodeling, etc.?

Words cannot describe how God showed up. As soon as I became pastor, I was contacted by Forestville Baptist Church in Greenville. There was a staff member there who knew my ministry and understood my call. Their desire was to build a partnership with us and to help us in numerous ways. I could spend much time writing pages and pages on how God blessed us. By accepting this call, God has used Laurel Baptist Church in opening many doors of opportunity to help other churches have hope, revitalize their churches and to write this book entitled "Spiritual Strokes." You see, Laurel Baptist Church had a stroke — a spiritual stroke. No, this is not a mega church, nor is it a large church (yet). However, we are out of debt, thousands have been spent to renovate the facilities. We do have a pastor, minister of education, worship leader, ACTS ministry director, minister of students, Hispanic pastor, secretary, and two musicians. The church is organized, sanctified, excited and motivated. At this time, God has opened the door for me to help in revitalizing eleven other churches while pastoring Laurel Baptist Church. What a joy! When God completes my work here as a pastor, I trust this church will continue to go forward.

Laurel Baptist Church realized they had suffered several spiritual strokes. They have dealt with their spiritual blood clots, and there is joy in focusing on God, His Great Commission, prayer, evangelism, discipleship, fellowship, ministry and worship. Friend, God can and does open doors. By examining this church at Philadelphia, we can understand why the moving of the Spirit of God came upon these believers and set before them an open door. According to verse 1, though they had little strength, the Master said they had kept His Word and had not denied His name.

Think about the open doors God has for you in your church. Every church has the opportunity to proclaim the Gospel. When Paul the apostle recognized the open door, he seized that opportunity to serve his Lord. The church at Philadelphia may have been a small congregation and, according to the world's standards, was a weak church. We may be weak, but He is strong! In Hebrews 11:34, after reading of the great men and women of the faith, we are told that *"out of weakness [they] were made strong."*

This church at Philadelphia kept God's Word by believing it and obeying it. Satan has hindered the work of God in many churches. He has discouraged, hindered and frustrated the church today. May we, as His Church, refuse to deny the name of the Lord and be determined by the help of the Holy Spirit to be faithful as we approach the soon return of Christ.

Let us remember that our Lord is holy; therefore, we should seek to be holy, for He is holy (1 Peter 1:6). Our Lord is true, for Christ is the only truth. As a church seeks revitalization, may the congregation remember *"He that hath the key of David"* controls everything. He opens, He shuts, and He has all the authority in heaven and earth. Our God is able to turn things around in our churches if we will seek to be like the church at Philadelphia.

If we will confess our failures, our sins, our weaknesses and our inabilities, God Himself will handle the satanic forces. He will, by His power, subdue the enemy before our eyes — not only now, but in the future.

Jesus said, *"Behold I come quickly: hold that fast which thou hast, that no man take thy crown" (Revelation 3:11)*. Christ is coming again! Let us hold fast to those things that are pleasing to God. May we dedicate ourselves and return to those essentials that build up the church. Let us return to our first love by being faithful to Bible teaching, evangelism, discipleship and missions.

The church at Philadelphia had no spiritual blood clots. They were sold out to Christ; therefore, they received the promises and blessings of God. Your church can have these same experiences by confessing and repenting of the spiritual blood clot of sin: *"If we confess our sins, he is faithful and just to forgive us our sins, and to cleanse us from all unrighteousness" (1 John 1:9)*.

It is so exciting to know that God can and will open the doors for us. He is ready. Are you?

"He that hath an ear, let him hear what the Spirit saith unto the churches." (Revelation 3:13)

CHAPTER FOURTEEN

OVERCOMING SPIRITUAL STROKES
PSALM 51:12

"Restore unto me the joy of thy salvation; and uphold me with thy free spirit." (Psalm 51:12)

Throughout the previous chapters, we have discovered that churches and individual Christians can experience strokes in the spiritual realm just as one can in the physical realm. A stroke is a terrible thing, resulting in paralysis and even death.

The good news in all of this is that we have a Great Physician — and not only can He help us overcome a stroke, but He is also able to do exceeding and abundantly more than we could ever ask or think! We can experience the joy of our salvation once again!

When I look back over the some twenty or more years after my dad's stroke, I realize that as a result of the doctors, hospitals and medicines, he was able to walk again, drive again, feed himself again, dress himself again, and enjoy life. Now, as a pastor, I understand that God Himself is able to completely heal us and make us even stronger than before our spiritual stroke.

Many examples could be used to describe such churches; however, one church stands out in my mind. That church is the

First Baptist Church of Woodstock, Georgia, where Dr. Johnny Hunt pastors. You should read of his testimony concerning his call to this church. It was a terrible situation indeed, with some three-hundred-plus people attending. It was filled with spiritual blood clots and had suffered spiritual strokes. Today, First Baptist Church of Woodstock is one of the largest churches in the Southern Baptist Convention.

God can turn any church around and empower the church to have her greatest days ever. In order for this to be a reality, however, there are certain things every church must do. Understand that I have never pastored a mega church. It has never been my desire. What I love to do is to go into a church where the believers understand that they have experienced a spiritual stroke, and where they truly desire to see God show up and begin to move within their midst. It is somewhat hard to believe, but there are churches that have settled for the status quo and are content with their stroke and are just waiting to die.

Many Christians and churches are like the man I once knew who was a member of my church. This man had emphysema as a result of his many years of smoking. His problem became so severe that he required an oxygen tank. Eventually he was placed on our homebound list. One day I visited his home. When I knocked on his front door, he called out to me and asked that I come to the back door. He was physically unable to come to the door. After entering his back door, there he was, sitting in his chair with his oxygen tank and next to his ashtray that contained some thirty to forty cigarette butts.

Like this man, many of our churches that have suffered spiritual strokes will not change because they are satisfied being spiritually sick and are on life support. They have one foot in the grave and the other foot on a banana peel. Some are close to having the death rattle, yet they will not change.

My friend, there are some basic things we can do to overcome our spiritual strokes and have us moving in the right direction for victory, revival and success. If we follow these simple, basic steps, God will heal us and bless us.

First and foremost, a church must return to the Word of God. Almost all Baptist churches claim to be people of the Book, but the truth is, we are far from it. Just look around most churches and you will discover that many never open their Bibles at church services. Most leaders know more about bylaws than they do about the Bible. As a young boy growing up in a troubled church, I remember a certain deacon who would come to the business meetings with bylaws folded in his back pocket. Without looking at the bylaws, he could quote page 2, paragraph 3 under article 4. This man and his wife kept our church on pins and needles. Oh yes, our church believed in the Bible, but I believe the bylaws had preeminence over the Bible. I have discovered over the years that a preacher is to simply open the Bible and preach the Word, in season and out of season. Stay with the Book! Preach expository sermons verse by verse. Feed the sheep. When this is done, those who love the Word will feed on the Word, and those who attend for any other purpose will either get right with God or leave.

I'd like to repeat a story I shared earlier in this book about an elderly preacher who was raised on a farm. Learn from this wise old preacher. By understanding what he was saying, you will know where to begin revitalizing your life, your class, and your church. When he was a boy, his father had one chore for him to do every night before going to bed. It was his responsibility to go out to the barn and check on a cow in one of the stalls. The old preacher said he noticed that every time he took his lantern into the barn and the light would shine, two things would always happen: The birds in the old barn would begin to sing, and the rats would run for cover. After becoming a preacher of the Gospel, he also noticed when he entered a worship service, opened his Bible and began to preach, the Word of God (which is the Light) would shine. As a result, two things would always happen: The Christians would begin to sing, and the rats would still run for cover. Amen! It is amazing how we boast about being people of the Book, yet the Bible is completely left out of our decision-making process. Today, everyone has an opinion, and we go by people's opinions and popularity when we make our choices. It is no wonder why we are suffering from blood clots and spiritual strokes.

Second, the church must choose leaders who stand on the Word of God. When a church leader will not stand with the pastor on the Word of God, that leader will fight the pastor on everything. If this is the case, what should the pastor do? He is to keep preaching the Word, verse by verse, chapter by chapter. Love the Lord and preach Jesus! Over time the Holy Spirit will do His work. Either hearts will be changed, or God Himself will step in and remove that person. A good example of this is found in an Old Testament text. In Numbers 16:1-3, Moses and Aaron were God's chosen men to lead His people. In these verses, we read where Korah rebelled against Moses and Aaron to exercise authority. Like many of our churches that suffer from spiritual strokes, Korah and others protested against God's chosen and refused to follow their leadership. Moses made it clear that God had separated them, brought them near to the Lord, and had given those He had appointed to minister to the congregation. Moses asked them this question in verse 10: *"And seek ye the priesthood also?"* Moses realized that what they were doing was rebellion against God and continued by saying, *"Thou and all thy company are gathered together against the Lord: and what is Aaron that ye murmur against him?"* (Numbers 16:11). Here was hatred against God's authority and rebellion against God.

What does Numbers 16 teach us? This chapter teaches us that God's people will know the man of God, that God's power will handle the situation, and that God's purging will bring about fear and respect toward the will of God. If we in the Church are to overcome spiritual strokes, then let us gladly accept the place we have been assigned to and submit to those over us, according to the Word of God. We can then begin to experience a smooth and properly functioning body of Christ.

The greatest spiritual blood thinner in removing spiritual

blood clots is the Word of God. Don't forget, you were saved by the Word of God, *"Being born again, not of corruptible seed, but of incorruptible, by the Word of God, which liveth and abideth for ever"* *(1 Peter 1:23)*. In the Psalms, we are told that we are blessed when we delight in the law of the Lord (1:2). Joy comes from the Word, because the joy of the Lord is our strength.

If we truly seek God with our whole heart, He will help us rebuild the spiritual walls of our church. He can heal our situations, cleanse us (Psalm 119:9), open our eyes by removing the spiritual cataracts from our eyes, and quicken us according to His Word (Psalm 119:25). Allow our Lord to clean out your eyes with His spiritual eyesalve. Return to your first love. His Word will revive and lift you up. God will remove all spiritual blood clots. Bless His Holy Name!

CPSIA information can be obtained at www.ICGtesting.com
Printed in the USA
LVOW10s0754071015

457076LV00001B/2/P